6/19
4

D1261930

BENJAMIN
FRANKLIN

MARY ELIZABETH SALZMANN

Consulting Editor, Diane Craig, M.A./Reading Specialist

Super Sandcastle

An Imprint of Abdo Publishing
abdopublishing.com

abdopublishing.com

Published by Abdo Publishing, a division of ABDO, PO Box 398166, Minneapolis, Minnesota 55439. Copyright © 2017 by Abdo Consulting Group, Inc. International copyrights reserved in all countries. No part of this book may be reproduced in any form without written permission from the publisher. Super SandCastle™ is a trademark and logo of Abdo Publishing.

Printed in the United States of America, North Mankato, Minnesota
062016
092016

Editor: Rebecca Felix
Content Developer: Nancy Tuminelly
Cover and Interior Design and Production: Mighty Media, Inc.
Photo Credits: barockschloss/Flickr; Library of Congress; Mighty Media, Inc.; Shutterstock; Wellcome Library, London; Wikimedia Commons

Library of Congress Cataloging-in-Publication Data
Names: Salzmann, Mary Elizabeth, 1968- author.
Title: Benjamin Franklin / by Mary Elizabeth Salzmann ; consulting editor,
  Diane Craig, M.A./Reading Specialist.
Description: Minneapolis, Minnesota : Abdo Publishing, [2017] | Series:
  Scientists at work
Identifiers: LCCN 2015050525 (print) | LCCN 2016002512 (ebook) | ISBN
  9781680781571 (print) | ISBN 9781680776003 (ebook)
Subjects: LCSH: Franklin, Benjamin, 1706-1790--Juvenile literature. |
  Statesmen--United States--Biography--Juvenile literature. |
  Scientists--United States--Biography--Juvenile literature. |
  Inventors--United States--Biography--Juvenile literature. |
  Printers--United States--Biography--Juvenile literature.
Classification: LCC E302.6.F8 S257 2016 (print) | LCC E302.6.F8 (ebook) | DDC
  973.3092--dc23
LC record available at http://lccn.loc.gov/2015050525

Super SandCastle™ books are created by a team of professional educators, reading specialists, and content developers around five essential components—phonemic awareness, phonics, vocabulary, text comprehension, and fluency—to assist young readers as they develop reading skills and strategies and increase their general knowledge. All books are written, reviewed, and leveled for guided reading, early reading intervention, and Accelerated Reader™ programs for use in shared, guided, and independent reading and writing activities to support a balanced approach to literacy instruction.

CONTENTS

A MAN OF MANY TALENTS

Benjamin Franklin was a **Founding Father**. He was a writer. He was an inventor and scientist too.

Benjamin Franklin is on the $100 bill.

BENJAMIN FRANKLIN

BORN: January 17, 1706, Boston, Massachusetts

MARRIED: Deborah Read, September 1, 1730 (common-law marriage)

CHILDREN: William Franklin, Francis Folger Franklin, Sarah Franklin Bache

DIED: April 17, 1790, Philadelphia, Pennsylvania

EARLY YEARS

Benjamin grew up in Boston, Massachusetts. He left school at age 10. School cost money. His parents could no longer afford it.

A view of Boston from the ocean in the 1700s

Benjamin went to work with his father. They made soap and candles.

Then Benjamin worked for his brother James. James was a printer. He taught Benjamin to be a printer too.

Benjamin often read books. He learned math and **grammar** this way.

Benjamin working as a printer

MOVE TO PHILADELPHIA

Franklin left Boston at age 17. He went to Philadelphia, Pennsylvania. He became a shopkeeper and bookkeeper.

A map of Philadelphia in the 1700s

Benjamin later returned to printing. He **published** the *Pennsylvania Gazette* in 1729. It was a newspaper. He wrote a book years later called *Poor Richard's Almanack*.

A cartoon from the Pennsylvania Gazette

Franklin started America's first library. It is the Library Company of Philadelphia. It opened in 1731. It is still open today.

FRANKLIN THE INVENTOR

Franklin invented many things. One was a new kind of **fireplace**. He invented it in 1742. It heated a room better. It also let less smoke into the room.

Franklin called it the "Pennsylvania fireplace." Later it was called the "Franklin stove."

Wood burning in a Franklin stove

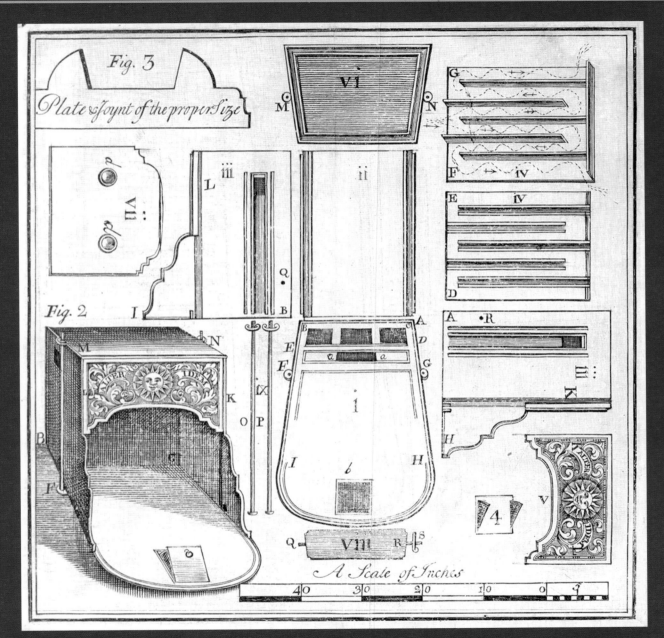

Franklin's original drawing for the Franklin stove

THE LIGHTNING ROD

Franklin also made an invention for buildings.

Lightning often hits tall buildings. This can cause **damage**. Franklin created a lightning rod. It would prevent damage.

A lightning rod
is a metal pole.
It is put on top
of a building.
A wire goes
from the pole
to the ground.
Lightning hits the
pole. It follows
the wire. It hits
the ground.
It doesn't hit
the rest of the
building.

FRANKLIN THE SCIENTIST

Franklin experimented with electricity. People thought lightning was electric. But this hadn't been proven. Franklin wanted to prove it. His ideas became famous.

A painting of Franklin in 1759

Sometimes lightning strikes sideways.

BIG IDEAS

Franklin's first idea was to stand on a building holding a metal pole. This pole would work like a lightning rod. Other scientists tested this idea. But it was **dangerous**. Electricity moves through metal. Lightning hurt some people who did this experiment.

Franklin had another idea. He thought using a kite would be safer. A kite could fly very high. The scientist could stay on the ground. And he or she would not have to touch metal.

ELECTRIC EXPERIMENT

Franklin's idea was to fly a kite with a metal frame during a storm. A metal key would be tied to its string. A wire would go from the key to a Leyden jar. This is a special jar. It stores electricity.

Leyden jars from the 1700s

Franklin would hold the kite as it flew near the storm. Lightning would hit the metal frame. It would move down the string to the key. Then it would move down the wire into the jar. This would prove lightning is electric!

ADVANCING SCIENCE

Some people think Franklin never did the kite experiment. Others believe he did. Either way, his experiment became famous. And it led to more experiments with electricity.

Franklin's ideas helped advance science and technology.

MORE ABOUT FRANKLIN

Franklin was a musician. He also played CHESS.

Franklin wrote all his life. He helped write the DECLARATION OF INDEPENDENCE.

Franklin DIDN'T PATENT his inventions. He felt people should share their inventions freely.

TEST YOUR KNOWLEDGE

1. How old was Franklin when he left school?

2. Franklin invented a lightning rod. *True or false?*

3. What was tied to the string in Franklin's kite experiment?

THINK ABOUT IT!

Have you ever had an electric shock? What did it feel like?

ANSWERS: 1. 10 2. True 3. Key

GLOSSARY

damage – harm or ruin.

dangerous – able or likely to cause harm or injury.

fireplace – an opening in a wall where you can build a fire.

Founding Father – a man who played an important part in creating the US government.

grammar – the rules for the proper way to write and speak a language.

publish – to prepare and produce written text to sell.